*"Poetry isn't someth[...]
of life; it is at the c[...]
We turn to poetry to help us
understand or cope with our
most intense experiences"*

Carol Ann Duffy,
Poet Laureate

Thank you

Thanks, first of all, to all our poets, who gave permission for us to reproduce their work virtually on a telephone call. We are delighted to be able to include works by the *Poet Laureate, Carol Ann Duffy*; by *Kathleen Jamie*; by the UK's grand old man of poetry, *Edwin Morgan*; and by America's most popular poet, *Billy Collins*. And we are also pleased to provide a platform for a new generation of budding poets, the winners of our first poetry competition.

Thanks also to our sponsors the Miller Group and Cardew Group, who covered all costs to guarantee that every penny of the cover price goes to the Foundation....

Thanks to our editor, Aileen Ballantyne; and also to our competition judges, in particular to Robert Alan Jamieson, poet, novelist, chair of the judges, and lecturer in Creative Writing at Edinburgh University; and to poet and novelist Diana Hendry for her invaluable advice and a "second eye."

Thanks also to Navyblue, our design agency who donated their time and expertise, and to Hamish Whyte, publisher and poet, for help, suggestions and advice at every turn and also to Lizzie MacGregor of the Scottish Poetry Library.

Thanks to Harvey Dingwall and his fellow artists at the Edinburgh College of Art who produced original artwork against deadlines many would have regarded as impossible.

Bringing your gifts together by using the funds raised through the sale of this book the Sick Kids Friends Foundation will be able to support sick children and their families, providing extra medical equipment, family accommodation and comforts.

You don't have to be a doctor to help sick kids get better... together you have done it with the magic of the pen and brush!

Maureen Harrison
Chief Executive,
The Sick Kids Friends Foundation

As a novelist, I've always been envious of poets -
they can say in a few words or lines something
that might take me hundreds of pages to replicate.
They are more akin to magicians than storytellers.

In this book you'll find feats of magic from poets
new and established, in both English and Scots.
You'll encounter birth, childhood and the wonder
of Christmas. It's a book you can share, a book
you can devour in one sitting, or dip into through
the rest of your life. And remember - these brilliant
writers gave their words free of charge, so every
purchase benefits a first-rate Scottish charity,
the Sick Kids Friends Foundation.

I hope you'll read on and be spellbound.
I hope you'll buy copies for your friends and family.
Thank you for helping sick kids get better.

Ian Rankin

A Child's Sleep

I stood at the edge of my child's sleep
hearing her breathe;
although I could not enter there,
I could not leave.

Her sleep was a small wood,
perfumed with flowers;
dark, peaceful, sacred,
acred in hours.

And she was the spirit that lives
in the heart of such woods;
without time, without history,
wordlessly good.

I spoke her name, a pebble dropped
in the still night,
and saw her stir, both open palms
cupping their soft light;

then went to the window. The greater dark
outside the room
gazed back, maternal, wise,
with its face of moon.

Carol Ann Duffy

The Wishing Tree

"One day walking in
Argyll with my husband
we encountered a wishing
tree which surprised us a
great deal because I didn't
know there were any in
Scotland. I mean a tree
people have bashed coins
into for a wish or a desire -
I knew they existed in
Ireland but had never
seen one in Scotland."

I stand neither in the wilderness
nor fairyland,

but in the fold
of a green hill,

the tilt from one parish
into another.

To look at me
through a smirr of rain

is to taste the iron
in your own blood;

because I bear
the common currency

of longing: each wish
each secret assignation.

My limbs lift, scabbed
with greenish coins

I draw into my slow wood
fleur-de-lys, the enthroned Britannia.

Behind me, the land
reaches towards the Atlantic.

And though I'm poisoned
choking on the small change

of human hope
daily beaten into me

look: I am still alive –
in fact, in bud.

Kathleen Jamie

Bairnsang

Wee toshie man,
       gean tree and rowan
gif ye could staun
yer feet wad lichtsome tread
granite and saun,
but ye cannae yet staun
sae maun courie tae ma airm
an greetna, girna, Gretna Green

Peedie wee lad
       saumon, siller haddie
gin ye could rin
ye'd rin richt easy-strang
ower causey an carse,
but ye cannae yet rin
sae maun jist courie in
and fashna, fashna, Macrahanish Sand

Bonny wee boy
       peeswheep an whaup
gin ye could sing, yer sang
wad be caller
as a lauchin mountain burn
but ye cannae yet sing
sae maun courie tae ma hert
an grieve nat at aa, Ainster an Crail

My ain tottie bairn
    sternie an lift
gin ye could daunce, yer daunce
wad be that o life itsel,
but ye cannae yet daunce
sae maun courie in my erms
and sleep, saftly sleep, Unst and Yell

Kathleen Jamie

Innocence

They leap and spin and shout
brash daubs of yellow red and blue
they loop the loop they hula hoop
turn somersaults and cartwheels
on the canvas of an endless day.
A simple bliss – you've not yet learnt
to mix a realistic grey and so
no clouds obscure your pure clear sky.
Only on the sun's grin a mistake –
the smudge of your purple thumb.

Dilys Rose

Glasgow

In the tram with my mother –
I was five or six –
drunk man leaned across
offered me a sixpence.
'Ur ye a good boay?
Sure ye're a good boay.'
I was not so sure.
My mother hissed
'Take it, take it,
always take
what a drunk man gives you!'
I remember how nicely
he clasped my hand round the coin.

Edwin Morgan

When Lying on our Bellies was Brilliant

When one of you burst out of the other
my body butterflied, lightshod hoofbeats
skedaddled from the hubbub for cover,
and we gawped at one another like triplets.
Now the sky's vermilion chills to cool,
and time cuts with brusque abbreviations,
keep in mind when lying on our bellies
was brilliant, when starlings whirled the rose sky.

We opened to all six pearlwort eyes
and jabbled and jibbled through the glades
and wild garlic, as a galaxy of dragonflies
lig-lagged and dizzied the lint-bells and heather
and cool winds absolved the coastline's ablations,
foxtails shushing below the balefires' lilac
where bluehawks birled a spree, hinting the sky,
whose buffets reaved the tummocks
and ripple-grass, away under the weather,
and our arms, stretched wide, reached out forever.

Alan Gillis

The Land of Counterpane

When I was sick and lay a-bed,
I had two pillows at my head,
And all my toys beside me lay,
To keep me happy all the day.

And sometimes for an hour or so
I watched my leaden soldiers go,
With different uniforms and drills,
Among the bed-clothes, through the hills;

And sometimes sent my ships in fleets
All up and down among the sheets;
Or brought my trees and houses out,
And planted cities all about.

I was the giant great and still
That sits upon the pillow-hill,
And sees before him, dale and plain,
The pleasant land of counterpane.

Robert Louis Stevenson

Histories of Desire

That was when I threw the stone and then ran after;
splashing into Smallholme Burn I made the colours
of a summer's day cascade around me.

That was when the water stilled to rowanberries, clouds
and dark green leaves I could never reach before.
I tried to pick one up –
that was when the earth and sky first slipped
between my fingers.

All histories are histories of desire, they tell me
how my life begins and ends: a stretch of water,
a stone a child sends skimming
to the other side.

Ron Butlin

Gap Year

(for Mateo)

I

I remember your Moses basket before you were born.
I'd stare at the fleecy white sheet for days, weeks,
willing you to arrive, hardly able to believe
I would ever have a real baby to put in the basket.

I'd feel the mound of my tight tub of a stomach,
and you moving there, foot against my heart,
elbow in my ribcage, turning, burping, awake, asleep.
One time I imagined I felt you laugh.

I'd play you Handel's _Water Music_ or Emma Kirkby
singing Pergolesi. I'd talk to you, my close stranger,
call you Tumshie, ask when you were coming to meet me.
You arrived late, the very hot summer of eighty-eight.

You had passed the due date string of eights,
and were pulled out with forceps, blue, floury,
on the fourteenth of August on Sunday afternoon.
I took you home on Monday and lay you in your basket.

II

Now, I peek in your room and stare at your bed
hardly able to imagine you back in there sleeping,
your handsome face – soft, open. Now you are eighteen,
six foot two, away, away in Costa Rica, Peru, Bolivia.

I follow your trails on my _Times Atlas:_
from the Caribbean side of Costa Rica to the Pacific,
the baby turtles to the massive leatherbacks.
Then on to Lima, to Cuzco. Your grandfather

rings: 'Have you considered altitude sickness,
Christ, he's sixteen thousand feet above sea level.'
Then to the lost city of the Incas, Macchu Picchu,
where you take a photograph of yourself with the statue

of the original Tupac. You are wearing a Peruvian hat.
Yesterday in Puno before catching the bus for Copacabana
you suddenly appear on a webcam and blow me a kiss,
you have a new haircut; your face is grainy, blurry.

Seeing you, shy, smiling, on the webcam reminds me
of the second scan at twenty weeks, how at that fuzzy
moment back then, you were lying cross-legged with
an index finger resting sophisticatedly on one cheek.

You started the Inca trail in Arctic conditions
and ended up in subtropical. Now you plan the Amazon
in Bolivia. Your grandfather rings again to say
'There's three warring factions in Bolivia, warn him

against it. He canny see everything. Tell him to come home.'
But you say all the travellers you meet rave about Bolivia. You want
to see the Salar de Uyuni,
the world's largest salt-flats, the Amazonian rainforest.

And now you are not coming home till four weeks after
your due date. After Bolivia, you plan to stay
with a friend's Auntie in Argentina.
Then – to Chile where you'll stay with friends of Diane's.

And maybe work for the Victor Jara Foundation.
I feel like a home-alone mother; all the lights
have gone out in the hall, and now I am
wearing your large black slippers, flip-flopping

into your empty bedroom, trying to imagine you
in your bed. I stare at the photos you send by messenger:
you on the top of the world, arms outstretched, eager.
Blue sky, white snow; you by Lake Tararhua, beaming.

My heart soars like the birds in your bright blue skies.
My love glows like the sunrise over the lost city.
I sing along to Ella Fitzgerald, *A tisket A tasket*.
I have a son out in the big wide world.

A flip and a skip ago, you were dreaming in your basket.

Jackie Kay

Trio

Coming up Buchanan Street, quickly, on a sharp winter evening
a young man and two girls, under the Christmas lights -
The young man carries a new guitar in his arms,
the girl on the inside carries a very young baby,
and the girl on the outside carries a chihuahua.
And the three of them are laughing, their breath rises
in a cloud of happiness, and they pass
the boy says, 'Wait till he sees this but!'
The chihuahua has a tiny Royal Stewart tartan coat like a teapot-
    holder,
the baby in its white shawl is all bright eyes and mouth like favours
    in a fresh sweet cake,
the guitar swells out under its milky plastic cover, tied at the neck
    with silver tinsel tape and a brisk sprig of mistletoe.
Orphean sprig! Melting baby! Warm chihuahua!
Whether Christ is born, or is not born, you
put paid to fate, it abdicates
                        under the Christmas lights.
Monsters of the year
go blank, are scattered back,
can't bear this march of three.
- And the three have passed, vanished in the crowd
(yet not vanished, for in their arms they wind
the life of men and beasts, and music,
laughter ringing round them like a guard)
at the end of this winter's day.

Edwin Morgan

Nativity

The sun didn't leave us -
it was you and I who strayed,
in staying here sparking our candles,
not migrating with the birds.

Light refugees, bent cowering,
mourning summer's stateless flight.

Now a new year's being born,
string a starry hope across your mind.
Sacred cow slow, the baby awakes,

and wise folk with great gifts,
fools who leave their flocks
to follow cosmic glitter, all
who trust to Providence,
welcome the child alike.

Robert Alan Jamieson

The Blue of Mary's Dress

It is the blue that comes into its own light
with the eyes of the sunset.

It is the blue of the wilful
carols of the wind-chime;

it is not the colour of rainwater
nor is it described by ice or cornflower,

nor the hint of tide-less mist reverting
to estuary; though it is defined

against the ochre patience of horses
and the obstinate grey of a heron.

It is opaque, but as translucent as a baby
who is not yet born, one gently

unfolding, a child willing to lead
lions. Winter and the mother wait,

the world shudders in fear,
even the birdcall freezes.

But all that falls is an episode,
a revolution of the earth –

so, the children, wild as the sparrows,
laugh again torrents to tally days;

so, the garden has clapped its hands
into a willow-pattern, bearing gifts –

a bridge, a crooked fence,
a temple, nativities of apples,

pairs of birds agreeing Allelujahs;
this is the very shade of Mary's dress.

Dawn Wood

Christmas and Children in Sialkot, Pakistan

(as I remember celebrating it in the 1960s)

Blessings on the big day.
(bare din mumbarak ho)

a bowl of steaming rice
see it cooking in the courtyard
ladled out a Christmas taste
for the children of the compound
never mind the dirt and flies
it makes a feast, a concert

for Christmastime brings cold winds
from Kashmir and storms of rain
but today the sun shines gently
and the goat-stew curried gravy
simmers with potatoes
carrots and tomatoes.
let's lick our lips again

halleluya
beat the _tabla_
sweep the house
a bright _dopatta_
coloured clothes
with tinselled border

spangly shoes from the bazaar
fresh milk from the buffalo
shawl washed at the river bank
hair washed at the common pump
fetch the baby, run and follow

sing psalms and clap hands
dogs and donkeys flick their ears
the camel kneels
the vulture wheels
we live for the day today
sweetmeats and jamboree
jerseys given from charity
sit in shade beneath the trees

Santa Claus is nothing here
chimneys, candles, twigs of fir
presents, dancing, parties.
Here it's staving off hunger
hope of cure
for dysentery, malaria
hope that grain-growing weather
give us lentils and chapatis

sugar cane is in the fields
sweet and sticky, juicy yields
irrigation channels flow
chrysanthemums and dahlias
in pots on verandas
poinsettia bushes glow

new life, new sun
divine become human
earth blessed anew
we accept and know
this is somehow true.

Tessa Ransford

The Shepherd
Tells his Grandchild

That night as usual, it was cold.
You don't yet know how sharp
The frost can be on those hills.
We'd got the fire alight
And gathered a great pile of wood
To keep the wolves away
And warm the marrow of our bones
In the dire watches around two o'clock.

That night as usual, we were curled
In winter cloaks as close
To the fire as we could
But none of us was able to sleep
And in the fold the sheep
Were strangely restless –
A constant shuffling and bleating.

That night as usual, we thought first
That a wolf was about.
Cursing, we went to check the gates
And calm the flock
But we found nothing untoward
Though the sheep would not be stilled.

And now we too felt the air strangely
Pregnant with awe.
Suddenly a star blazed –
One we'd never seen before –
And the whole Milky Way started singing.

Elizabeth Birchall

Questions for Christmas

Will there be a child this year?
    Unexpectedly.

Are the wise men on their way?
    After a map-reading course.

Are the shepherds watching?
    As always.

Will the donkey nuzzle my hand?
    Sugar-lump or not.

Will there be snow and carols and an orange
at the bottom of my stocking and a Christmas tree?
    All of the above.

With lights?
    Clear ones.

Will there be love?
    Yes.

Diana Hendry and Hamish Whyte

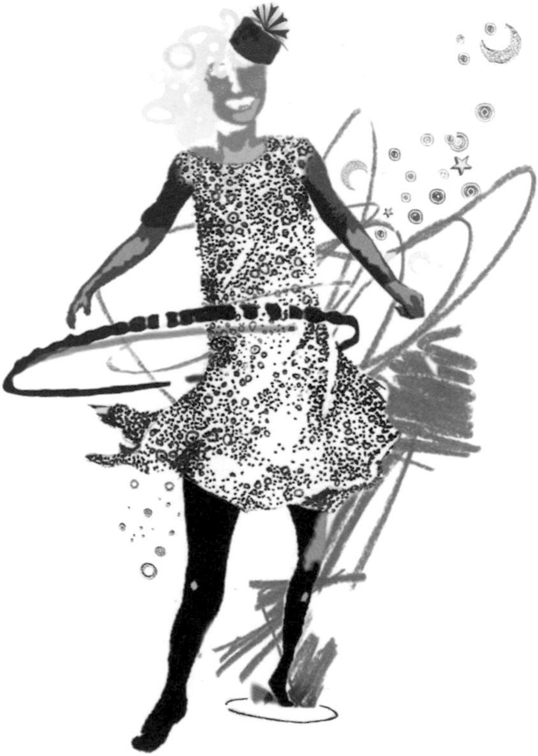

Liquorice Hoop

The Signet Library, Christmas 2008

We came fae the kirk tae the Signet:
through the haar o an Edinbro nicht
tae the doorway ahint auld St Giles:
the torches o flame were burnin in welcome
as we sat oorsels doun fir a feast.
Ah pit bids in fir aathin at raffle an auction -
well naebody minds fir bit bairns that are ill.

An it came tae the hour at the Signet
when coffee gans cauld in wee cups;
an fine siller spoons hit the sludge.
But juist as ah stairted tae gan doon the hall
past a thoosan auld books in their cages,
past slim Grecian pillars, sae graund an sae tall,
ma eye met the eye o Marilla the Hoola,
the star o the nicht in black silken tichts
wi her black-and-white liquorice hoop.
An ah minded the wecht o that auld hoola-hoop
an the twist o the waist that it took
tae set it tae spinnin juist richt -
then it seemed tae gan oan bi itsel.

Her English wis clear-cut as crystal:
a lady tae the tips o the white gloves she wore
an each gowd-spun hair o her heid.
She turned in her white-spotted frock
an gied me the black an white hoola tae try -

an ah was a boy o twinty again
pickin buckets o rasps at Blairgowrie
an eatin as mony as went in the pail:
their taste chert an sweet on ma palm,
an the scent o the lass at ma side as green
as thon day in the sun oan the ferm.

Ladeez and Gentlemen, this
is how it is done, she said;
ah turned oan ma heel,
an she gied me her haun wi a smile:
step up, step up, and hoola with me,
just step through the hoop, and you're young.

Aileen Ballantyne

Christmas Sparrow

The first thing I heard this morning
was a rapid flapping sound, soft, insistent -

wings against the glass as it turned out
downstairs when I saw the small bird
rioting in the frame of a high window,
trying to hurl itself through the enigma
of glass into the spacious light.

Then a noise in the throat of the cat
who was hunkered on the rug
told me how the bird had gotten inside,
carried in the cold night
through the flap of a basement door,
and later released from the soft grip of teeth.

On a chair, I trapped its pulsations
in a shirt and got it to the door,
so weightless it seemed
to have vanished into the nest of cloth.

But outside, when I uncupped my hands,
it burst into its element,
dipping over the dormant garden
in a spasm of wingbeats
then disappeared over a row of tall hemlocks.

For the rest of the day,
I could feel its wild thrumming
against my palms as I wondered about
the hours it must have spent
pent in the shadows of that room,
hidden in the spiky branches
of our decorated tree, breathing there
among the metallic angels, ceramic apples, stars of yarn,
its eyes open, like mine as I lie in bed tonight
picturing this rare, lucky sparrow
tucked into a holly bush now,
a light snow tumbling through windless dark.

Billy Collins

True story

I'm eight. I'm lying awake on Christmas Eve.
I hear the sleigh bells tingle through the air.
I pull the curtain back: there's nothing there,
I see no Santa Claus - but I believe.

Hamish Whyte

The Real Santa

Billy says that Santa hasnae got a sleigh
He says Santa gets here on the motorway
He says he's got a Santa Nav to tak him to the door
Cos he disnae hae a chimney on his hoose any more

Billy says Santa's sledge has been articulated
That reindeer power and red noses is far too outdated
Billy says he can go a thousand miles an hour
The lights are bright as daytime cos it's electric power

Billy says that Santa's got a jumbo jet plane
It comes aa the way fae Lapland an flies up oor lane
Wi elves on the wings throwin pressies doon the lums
An reindeer eating carrots and chattin tae their chums

Why does Billy tell me aa thae stupid lies?
His heid's fu o fairies, or mincemeat fae thae pies
Ah'm just goin tae lie here an kid on ah'm asleep
Till Santa's helicopter comes, ah'll no let oot a cheep.

Gordon Bell

Small town Christmas

Before the party we spend the afternoon
decorating the classroom,
while the sky grows dark through the long windows,
and the lights of the classroom
hang outside in the dark sky.

Frances Atkinson gets to help,
because she's tall, pinning up the paper chains
we'd made earlier, and the strings of milk bottle tops
washed, but still smelling a bit
and a yellow and purple accordion-pleated bell.

We are clearing the desks to the side of the room
for the games and dancing,
when Petrena Connor gets up on a desk
and pulls up her skirt
to show her paper nylon petticoat.

The boys stop for a second,
then go on running round with their arms out
being aeroplanes, till a fight breaks out.
Charles Anderson, a fat boy, who will become a policeman,
bends down to pick up a sausage roll, then screams for the teacher

because Frankie Rossiter has sneaked up behind him
and stuck a drawing pin in his bum.
'I wanted to see if it would burst, Miss', he says,
and the teacher lets him away with it,
but only because it's Christmas.

I'm putting my Mum's mince pies on a plate
though nobody wants to eat them because they're home-made,
when Jimmy Syme, who hates me, says,
'They're weird', and stamps on my foot.
But it was a good party.

Afterwards we go back down the street,
past the Christmas tree outside the hairdresser's
and the blue and red bottles in the chemist's window.
It is a cold night, with frost on the ground,
and above the streetlights, the stars.

Lindy Barbour

The Light Gatherer

When you were small, your cupped palms
each held a candlesworth under the skin,
enough light to begin

and as you grew
light gathered in you, two clear raindrops
in your eyes,
        warm pearls, shy,
in the lobes of your ears, even always
the light of a smile after your tears.

Your kissed feet glowed in my one hand,
or I'd enter a room to see the corner you played in
lit like a stage set,

        the crown of your bowed head spotlit.
When language came, it glittered like a river,
silver, clever with fish,

        and you slept
with the whole moon held in your arms for a night light
where I knelt watching.

        Light gatherer. You fell from a star
into my lap, the soft lamp at the bedside
mirrored in you,

and now you shine like a snowgirl.
a buttercup under a chin, the wide blue yonder
you squeal at and fly in,

        like a jewelled cave,
turquoise and diamond and gold, opening out
at the end of a tunnel of years.

Carol Ann Duffy

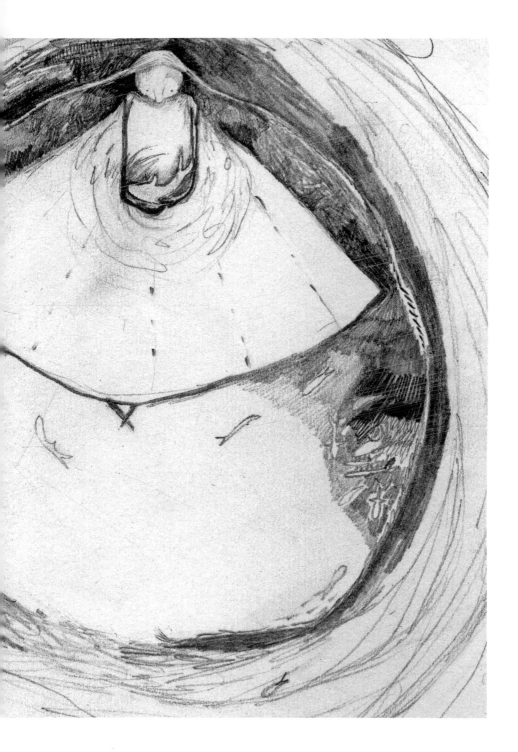

Carol Ann Duffy is the UK's first woman Poet Laureate and first Scottish-born Poet Laureate in the post's 341 year history. Born in Glasgow, she is Professor of Contemporary Poetry at Manchester Metropolitan University, and lives in Manchester with her daughter, Ella. It was Ella who encouraged her to take up the post of Poet Laureate, saying, "It's time a woman did it." An acclaimed poet, playwright and anthologist, she has received many of the major prizes for UK poetry, most recently the T.S. Eliot Prize, 2006 for *Rapture*. She was awarded the CBE in 2001. Among her most recent books are: *New and collected Poems for Children*, and *Mrs Scrooge*.

Edwin Morgan is regarded as one of the UK's greatest living poets and is Scotland's Poet Laureate. Born in Glasgow in 1920, he is recognised in particular for his inventiveness and range – neatly summed up by the name of his poetry collection published in 1973, entitled *From Glasgow to Saturn*. Endlessly innovative, Morgan has spent his life developing and refining new forms. It was Morgan's poem, with its first line: 'Open the Doors' which set the tone of the proceedings at the opening of the Scottish Parliament.

His work covers the whole range of human history, from twenty billion years BC to 9/11. His work also includes the theme of love in poems including 'Trio', 'Strawberries' and 'One Cigarette'. Aged ninety next year, his latest collections are *A Book of Lives*, (Carcanet) and *Dreams and Other Nightmares*, (Mariscat Press) – being published for 2010.

Billy Collins. Born in 1941, former American Poet Laureate and America's most popular poet is known for his ability to reveal the unexpected in what, at first glance, might seem quite "ordinary" subjects in his poems.

The Beat Poet Young Dawkins – who is also Vice Principal, Development and Alumni at Edinburgh University – writes: "One of the highlights of my poetry career has been to share a stage with Billy Collins. He is certainly the most popular American poet of this era. He is a charming, humorous and deeply thoughtful writer who touches gently yet firmly upon the common human condition. A great poet, and a kind man."

Kathleen Jamie is regarded as one of the leading contemporary poets in the UK. Her collections, *Jizzen* and *The Queen of Sheba* both won the Geoffrey Faber Memorial Award and her *Selected Poems, Mr and Mrs Scotland are Dead* was shortlisted for the International Griffin Poetry Award. She lectures in Creative Writing at St Andrews University and lives in Fife. In his introduction to Kathleen Jamie's recent "travel" book, *Findings*, Richard Mabey, author of *Flora Britannica* writes: "Kathleen Jamie is a supreme listener....And in the quietness of her listening, you hear her own voice: clear, subtle, respectful, and so unquenchably curious that it makes the world anew."

Ron Butlin is the Edinburgh Poet Laureate (Makar) and a prize-winning novelist. He lives in Edinburgh with his wife, the writer Regi Claire, and their golden retriever. "At some point when writing a poem, story or whatever, I am usually aware of going to back to a childhood memory or impression," he said, "even if only fleetingly. It is like touching base one last time before going into unknown territory."

His most recent books are: *No More Angels*, a collection of short stories, and the novel, *Belonging*, which was Book at Bedtime on BBC Radio 4. Next year sees the production of his new opera (with composer, Lyell Cresswell), *The Money Man*, for Scottish Opera. At present he is completing a new novel.

Jackie Kay was born and brought up in Scotland, Jackie Kay is a poet, and also writes for the stage and television. Her hilarious *Maw Broon Monologues* were premiered at The Tron in Glasgow in November 2009. Her poetry collections include *The Adoption Papers* (winner of a Forward Prize, a Saltire Award and a Scottish Arts Council Book Award). Her first novel, *Trumpet* won the Guardian Fiction Prize, a Scottish Arts Council Book Award and The Authors' Club First Novel Award. Her latest book is *The Lamplighter* (Bloodaxe, 2008). She is Professor of Creative Writing at Newcastle University.

Robert Alan Jamieson, chair of the competition judges, has been instrumental in the development of creative writing at the University of Edinburgh. He is the author of three novels, two collections of poetry and two plays, and has edited a number of anthologies.

His most recent publications are *Nort Atlantik Drift* and *The Cutting Down of Cutty Sark*. His new poem, 'Nativity', is being published in this anthology for the first time. He was born in Lerwick, Shetland on Up Helly Aa and grew up in the crofting community at Sandness. He attended the University of Edinburgh as a mature student and subsequently held the William Soutar Fellowship in Perth. He was a co-editor of *Edinburgh Review*, 1993-98, and writer in residence at the universities of Glasgow and Strathclyde, 1998-2001.

Biographies

Diana Hendry, poet and novelist, is a judge in this year's Carols for Christmas Poetry Competition. She has published more than forty books for children, including *Harvey Angell* which won a Whitbread Award in 1991 and *You Can't Kiss It Better*, set in Edinburgh (2003). Her third and most recent collection of poetry is *Late Love and Other Whodunnits*. Her 'Poem for a Hospital Wall' reprinted here was written when she was Writer in Residence at Dumfries & Galloway Royal Infirmary. Diana says, "It was written on an actual wall in the hospital by the artist Rachel Mimiec." Currently Diana is a Royal Literary Fund fellow at Edinburgh University.

Alan Gillis is an award-winning poet who lives in Edinburgh. The Irish poet Ciaran Carson says of Gillis's poetry: "I was immediately hooked by its linguistic exuberance, its intelligence, its black humour, its sometimes zany flights of imagination that are grounded in an emotional reality." Dr Gillis, who was born in Belfast, teaches Poetry and Creative Writing at the University of Edinburgh. His latest collection, *Hawks and Doves*, is a Poetry Book Society Recommendation and was shortlisted for the T.S. Eliot Prize.

Dilys Rose, is an award-winning poet and short story writer who also teaches Creative Writing at Edinburgh University. Awards include the first Macallan/Scotland on Sunday Short Story Prize and the RLS Memorial Award. Her recent publications include *Bodywork* and *Selected Stories*.
   Born and brought up in Glasgow, she has lived near the Royal Hospital for Sick Children for many years. "I have lived most of my adult life in Edinburgh, mostly in Tollcross which I mostly love. It's not always nice or easy but it's never boring. As a writer, it has kept me grounded. I still feel very lucky to have The Meadows almost on my doorstep. As for the Sick Kids', what parent wouldn't want to support it? Great to see a publication which celebrates such a special and necessary place."

Hamish Whyte, is a publisher (Mariscat Press) and poet. His latest collection is *A Bird in the Hand* (Shoestring Press). He recently edited *Kin: Scottish Poems about Family*, (SPL/Polygon). His pamphlet, *Christmasses* was published by Vennel Press in 1998. and he is Honorary Research Fellow in the Scottish Literature Department, Glasgow University. His poem 'True story' and 'Questions for Christmas' (written as a Christmas card, with Diana Hendry, above), are being published here for the first time.

Aileen Ballantyne is a former journalist with *The Sunday Times*, *The Guardian* and *The Scotsman* who has recently begun writing poetry. She won the Edinburgh University Sloan Prize for poetry while studying for an MSc in Creative Writing this year and is now studying for a PhD. 'Liquorice Hoop, The Signet Library, Christmas 2008' was written shortly after attending last year's dinner.

Competition Winners in the Anthology

Published
Poets' Category:

'The Blue of Mary's Dress' by
Dawn Wood (First)

'Christmas and Children
in Sialkot, Pakistan' by
Tessa Ransford, OBE (Runner up)

'The Shepherd Tells his Grandchild' by
Elizabeth Birchall (Third)

Unpublished
Poets' Category

'Small town Christmas' by
Lindy Barbour (First)

'The Real Santa' by
Gordon Bell (Runner up)

The illustrations are by students and staff of Edinburgh College of Art Illustration department, arranged by Harvey Dingwall

Front/Back Cover illustration
Harvey Dingwall

'Bairnsang'
Cate James

'Innocence'
Laura Davis

'The Land of Counterpane'
Jonathan Gibbs

'Histories of Desire'
Jim McBride

'Trio'
James Albon

'Nativity'
Harvey Dingwall

'Liquorice Hoop'
Matthew McCann

'Christmas Sparrow'
Kristyna Litten

'The Light Gatherer'
Gillian Chantier

The copyright of all poems is retained by the poet. Our grateful thanks are due to the poets who gave so freely of their talents, to Pan Macmillan, and to all the publishers below for generously allowing us to reproduce these poems.

Carol Ann Duffy
'A Child's Sleep' from *New Selected Poems* 1984-2004. (Picador, 2004).

Kathleen Jamie
'The Wishing Tree' from *The Tree House* (Picador 2004). The introductory comments quoted from Kathleen Jamie to this poem are from: http://www.poetryarchive.org/poetryarchive which also contains recordings of Jamie reading 'The Wishing Tree,' and other poems. Kathleen Jamie 'Bairnsang' from *Jizzen* (Picador, 1999).

Dilys Rose
'Innocence' from *Madame Doubtfire's Dilemma* (Chapman, 1989).

Edwin Morgan
'Glasgow' from 'Pieces of Me,' from *Edwin Morgan, Inventions of Modernity*, by Professor Colin Nicholson, (Manchester University Press, 2002).

Ron Butlin
'Histories of Desire' from *Without a Backward Glance* (Barzan Publications, 2005).

Alan Gillis
'When Lying on our Bellies was Brilliant' from *Somebody Somewhere*, (Gallery Press, 2004).

Diana Hendry
'Poem for a Hospital Wall' *Borderers* (Peterloo, 2001).

Jackie Kay
'Gap Year' from *Darling: New and Selected Poems* (Bloodaxe, 2007).

Edwin Morgan
'Trio' from *Edwin Morgan, Collected Poems* (Carcanet, 1996).

Billy Collins
'Christmas Sparrow' from *Nine Horses* (Picador 2003).

Carol Ann Duffy
'The Light Gatherer' from *Feminine Gospels* (Picador, 2002).

The quote from Carol Ann Duffy at the front of the book is from an interview in *The Times* newspaper on August 29, 2009.

Robert Louis Stevenson
Robert Louis Stevenson's 'The Land of Counterpane' has been a favourite at The Sick Kids Friends Foundation Carols for Christmas evening for many years. Robert Louis Stevenson (1850-1894) was born in Edinburgh's New Town and lived with his family at 17 Heriot Row. He used to play in Queen Street Gardens and could see a small pond known as Farmer Wood's cattle pond from his bedroom window. This pond is believed to have been the inspiration for Skeleton Island, an island in Robert Louis Stevenson's novel, *Treasure Island*, published in 1883.

Acknowledgments